'Accessible, full of common ... is supportive, helpful and wi... enable practitioners ... early years settings to become conf... ...better able to support children in their exploration and their choices around gender diversity, sexuality and life!

Early years settings will find practical ideas to make positive changes in thinking, practice, and attitudes and to be the best role models for all children and the very young children who are gender questioning.'
— *Clair Barnard, Early Childhood Project Co-ordinator*

'This is a must-read for early years practitioners who want to make a difference regarding gender diversity and sexuality, but aren't sure how or where to start. Real cases illuminate issues and dilemmas that are faced every day. Personal reflections and activities provoke changes in practitioners' thinking and practice. This book is engaging, it's inspiring and it's important.'
— *Mindy Blaise, Professor of Early Childhood Education,*
Victoria University, Australia

'*A Practical Guide to Gender Diversity and Sexuality in Early Years* makes an important contribution to scholarly debates, but perhaps more crucially, it provides vital insights and practical strategies for early childhood educators to work more effectively with children and their families. The writing is lively and engaging. It is a timely publication that draws on the author's extensive knowledge and expertise and offers a powerful space for asking and addressing pressing social justice questions.'
— *Dr Jayne Osgood PhD, Professor of Early Years and Gender,*
Centre for Education Research & Scholarship,
Middlesex University, London

'This is an important and timely book. Early years practitioners will find the practical ideas and activities invaluable in enabling them to think about gender and sexuality and to deepen the support they offer young children and their families.'
— *Kath Tayler, Senior Lecturer in Early Years Education,*
University of Brighton

of related interest

Can I tell you about Gender Diversity?
A guide for friends, family and professionals
CJ Atkinson
Illustrated by Olly Pike
ISBN 978 1 78592 105 6
eISBN 978 1 78450 367 3
Part of the Can I tell you about...? *series*

Who Are You?
The Kid's Guide to Gender Identity
Brook Pessin-Whedbee
Illustrated by Naomi Bardoff
ISBN 978 1 78592 728 7
eISBN 978 1 78450 580 6

Nurturing Personal, Social and Emotional Development in Early Childhood
A Practical Guide to Understanding Brain Development and Young Children's Behaviour
Debbie Garvey
Foreword by Dr Suzanne Zeedyk
ISBN 978 1 78592 223 7
eISBN 978 1 78450 500 4

Promoting Young Children's Emotional Health and Wellbeing
A Practical Guide for Professionals and Parents
Sonia Mainstone-Cotton
ISBN 978 1 78592 054 7
eISBN 978 1 78450 311 6

The Gender Agenda
A First-Hand Account of How Girls and Boys Are Treated Differently
Ros Ball and James Millar
Foreword by Marianne Grabrucker
ISBN 978 1 78592 320 3
eISBN 978 1 78450 633 9

Are You a Boy or Are You a Girl?
Sarah Savage and Fox Fisher
Illustrated by Fox Fisher
ISBN 978 1 78592 267 1
eISBN 978 1 78450 556 1

A Practical Guide to
GENDER DIVERSITY AND SEXUALITY
in Early Years

Deborah Price

Jessica Kingsley *Publishers*
London and Philadelphia

First published in 2018
by Jessica Kingsley Publishers
73 Collier Street
London N1 9BE, UK
and
400 Market Street, Suite 400
Philadelphia, PA 19106, USA

www.jkp.com

Library of Congress Cataloging in Publication Data
A CIP catalog record for this book is available from the Library of Congress

British Library Cataloguing in Publication Data
A CIP catalogue record for this book is available from the British Library

ISBN 978 1 78592 289 3
eISBN 978 1 78450 594 3

Printed and bound in the United States

I dedicate this book with love to two remarkable women in my life: my cousin Celina Mathieson and my sister-in-law Charlotte Lubert.

CONTENTS

ACKNOWLEDGMENTS

Central to this book, particularly the case studies, are all the children, families, practitioners and students I have worked with over many years. I am enormously grateful to them for sharing their stories. I would specifically like to thank Michaela Whiting, a student from the University of Brighton, Deborah Taylor from Roundabout nursery in Whitehawk, Brighton, and also Shaddai Tembo from Bristol Men in Early Years Network, for their thoughtful contributions.

Particular thanks must go to Judy Simon, a very experienced practitioner in Brighton who is committed to equalities practice and who provided much of the material for Chapter 5. Special thanks also to my colleague, writing partner and friend Kath Tayler, as I used many of the ideas that we discussed for our two books on LGBT diversity and gender diversity.

Additional grateful thanks to Fen Coles from Letterbox Library who has supported and advised me throughout. Similarly, thanks to Clair Barnard from the Early Childhood Project, Brighton. Thanks also to colleagues in the University of Brighton who have been supportive about LGBT diversity, especially the early years team. Mention must be made and thanks given to my co-writer and friend Dr Cathy Ota of Working With Others who inspired much of the writing on staff teams from our books on leadership and assertiveness.

Thanks, as ever, to Maria Jastrzebska who helped and supported me in numerous ways, but specifically with proofreading and thoughtful comments. And thanks to Allie Rogers, Sandi Fikuart, Nikki Sheehan, Suzanne Drew-Edwards, Lucy Cage and Lisa Heathfield: talented writers who allow me to regularly sit with them and read my work.

I am indebted to Stonewall, as always, whose website and publications have supported me throughout the book.

Finally I would like to give my thanks to Andrew James at Jessica Kingsley Publishers who had the confidence and insight to take this book forward to publication.

Chapter 1

INTRODUCTION

As a starting point for this book I ask you to think about some of the casual misuses of words concerning gender and sexuality that you might hear in a day. These are some of the ones that occurred to me:

- 'that's gay' in relation to anything
- 'man up' in telling someone to be stronger or more courageous
- 'you're doing that like a girl' in saying that it's being done at a low level.

I also wanted to share a story told to me by someone who was in a well-known shop that sells children's toys and equipment:

CASE STUDY 1.1: CHOOSING TOYS

Mother, to son: I'll buy you something, what would you like? How about this? (standing in front of car racing track)

Son (around age 3–5): (runs up to toy kitchen stuff) I want this!!

Mother: No, you can't have that girly cake mixer. Choose something else. Look over here.

Son: (now grabbing it and hugging it) But I want this!

Mother: Well you can't, stop being silly. Otherwise you can't have anything else.

REFLECTION
How did you feel reading this? Can you recognise yourself in this case study or anyone you know? If you are a parent I am sure that you, like me, have said things when under pressure and stress that you later regret. What would have been a more positive outcome to this incident?

The good practice that you carry out in your setting makes a difference. It is a positive environment in a world where there are too many instances of casual everyday gender stereotyping and homophobia. What you as an enlightened practitioner can provide is a respite from this relentless ongoing negative input that children and adults suffer from. Your setting can be somewhere that children will learn from the world that you offer them, and from you and your colleagues as role models, how to be a man or a woman in a positive and free way that allows them to grow up and express themselves openly.

The most important starting point in this book is that positive practice in thinking about gender diversity and sexuality is part of a wider picture of positive equalities work. Good equality and diversity practice should be the cornerstone of every practitioner's work. Every setting should be a completely inclusive experience for all children where they and their families feel welcomed and supported.

This starts with the families' and children's first steps into the setting.

ACTIVITY 1.1: FIRST IMPRESSIONS

As an exercise try to imagine a family's initial moments walking into a setting and think about what they might first see as they walk through the door. This is a good way to audit an early years setting. To make this exercise most effective think about it as stepping into the family's shoes by physically walking in the entrance of your setting. Also imagine this as a child and think about what could be seen from their height.

REFLECTION

The environment should be one that emphasises the diversity of the setting and the wider world. Families and children should be able to see representations of themselves and their lives around the setting and it should be obvious that all children's work is valued and displayed. This last is especially important, as children and families are more likely to build an attachment to a setting if they see their own families and lifestyles affirmed there.

Think about the feelings and reaction of a child coming to a setting and being unable to find any pictures on the wall or in any of the books that show themselves and their family positively. Families leaving their children in the settings should also be able to see them reflected in the setting so that they can truly believe that the setting recognises and affirms them. In this way the connections that the setting makes with the children and the families are strengthened.

Another important point is that it is not only in the relationships between the setting and the families and children that diversity and inclusion should be seen. This should also extend to the way that staff teams work and interact with each other. Relationships should be supportive and respectful and children should be able to see, as their roles models, adults who work with each other in a professional way. When we are thinking about the way that society is reflected in the microcosm that is the setting we can see that children should be able to view men and women caring for them in a variety of ways. This should be much more than women fulfilling the caring domestic roles and any male workers confined to playing in a more active way, for example always being in charge of outside sports.

This direction in adult interaction has to start with the manager and leader of the setting and cascade down. Because of this there is a section in this book on the manager's particular role in providing the impetus for an enhancement of practice and/or a change in direction for the setting. However, the manager can only lead and manage a team if they subscribe to the values and beliefs that are inherent in good gender diversity practice. The manager and leader have to win the hearts and minds of the team and they need to carry out the activities and ideas with conviction. Both men and women practitioners should be able to find useful information in this book and also feel that they are reflected in the case studies that are featured. The information and practices that are discussed are for all practitioners to think about and use to enhance their practice.

All of the above is part of positive equalities practice and gender diversity is included within this. Boys and girls should be able to see all of the things that they are interested in, all of the ways that they are within their families and wide-ranging images of the different ways to be boys and girls and men and women. This is also extended to families, who should be able to see a comprehensive and varied reflection of the richness of the wider world in terms of gender and roles reflected in the day-to-day practice of an early years setting. It is important for families to see themselves and their children reflected in the setting. It is also important to extend this by showing that there are a range of families and lifestyles as well. This is especially important if the setting is in an area where there is not much diversity.

A crucial point to make is that when we are talking about sexuality we are not talking about sex. We are talking about young children's future sexuality, their capacity for sexuality. Sexuality itself is a wide-ranging term that can include someone's ideas about their gender and their sexual orientation. The child today is the adult of tomorrow and we need to remember this as early years practitioners.

In this book you will find practical, real-life examples, case studies and ideas that will move your setting forward in its equality practice. The ideas and examples of practice have been taken from real working settings and have been used successfully by them. In the same way that Case Study 1.1 imagines the first impressions of a child and their family walking into a setting, the book will go through all aspects of an early years environment and think about it in terms of gender diversity. The book can be read from start to finish. It can also be used as an audit to work through, a tool to use to examine current practice and think about ways to move forward in all aspects of practice.

This book does deal with some challenging subjects, for example, the inclusion of LGB diversity and an examination of transgender awareness and support. The general ideas about gender might also be thought provoking if they contrast with the reader's deeply held beliefs about ways to be boys and girls, men and women. It is the intention within this book to start where the practitioner is and then, with a clear underpinning of theory and legislation, extend the range of thoughts about gender and the way that the setting can move forward in practice. This move forward can only happen if the practitioners truly understand why such practice is necessary and desirable.

Only when the adults in the setting make this essential shift in their thinking can the practice become part of the setting's everyday work. If practitioners carry out the activities and ideas about gender without fully understanding and agreeing with the theory and core reasoning behind the practices then the most positive effects will be lost.

By the end of the book every aspect of working with children in early years settings will be examined and analysed in terms of gender diversity.

Overview of the book

Chapter 2: Background to Legislation

This chapter gives an overview of key legislation that underpins our work around equalities in early years. This covers work with parents and as a staff team.

Chapter 3: The Manager

The thrust for outstanding equalities practice must come from the manager of a setting. In this chapter I look at how a manager can lead and inspire a team in this work. I examine what strategies they could use for encouraging positive attitudes towards equalities practice. This chapter also introduces the idea of mission statements and shows how effective they can be in making sure that equalities practice permeates every decision that is made in a setting.

Chapter 4: The Team and the Individual Practitioner in the Setting

This chapter draws on ideas that have been suggested by practitioners that will enhance practice within the team and show how good equalities practice can run through day-to-day activities and routines in a setting.

There are also some suggestions for team training and included are some example outlines of training for one hour, half a day and a full day.

Chapter 5: The Environment of the Setting and Ideas for Activities

This chapter examines and details a range of activities and ideas to carry out with children in the setting. There are also suggestions regarding the setting up of the environment and auditing what is already there.

Chapter 6: Supporting Families

This chapter discusses work with parents and considers good practice in terms of communication and interaction. Through case studies it also considers situations that can be difficult and proposes some solutions and strategies.

Chapter 7: LGB and Transgender Issues in Early Years

This chapter focuses on an often-overlooked aspect of equalities work in early years and thinks about LGBT work with children, staff and families. There is also a section on transgender and how this might impact on early years work.

Chapter 8: Conclusion

This chapter reflect on work done and considers ways forward.

Chapter 9: Resources

This chapter looks at resources that support the equalities work in a setting. Suggestions for books are also included and these include books suitable for children and also sources of information and further reading for staff members.

Conclusion

Finally I want to leave you with this thought about the nature of children and who they are. There are many theories about gender and its attributes and how this is manifested in young children.

> Think about any perceived differences between boys and girls and whether any differences might be due to biology such as hormonal and brain differences or due to the socialisation children receive within their families, early years settings and communities. While acknowledging the importance of both sides of this nature/nurture debate, you will then be asked to consider if there is another way of viewing this issue. Do children have their own power to challenge norms of gender behaviour or are there fixed truths about gender, which are beyond challenge? (Tayler and Price 2016: 10)

Chapter 2

BACKGROUND TO LEGISLATION

In this chapter we are going to specifically look at theory and legislation that concern gender, focusing on legislation. There are lots of books published that give the background to equalities theory and legislation. These would be good to look at for underpinning background material and I mention some in the resources section at the end of this book.

The main piece of legislation is the Equality Act 2010 and there is a very good overview that Acas have written which gives a clear perspective on the Act and can be found on their website (Acas n.d.). It doesn't especially mention early years but if you are a manager or leader reading this then you need to be aware that the Act also covers the rights of employees and the responsibilities of employers. There is also a very good simple guide to the Act: Government Equalities Office (2011).

Both of these guides are easily accessed and provide useful information that I don't need to repeat in this chapter. However, a very basic introduction to the Act is a good start to a discussion and the activity below would be an interesting piece of team training.

ACTIVITY 2.1: THE EQUALITY ACT

There are nine areas of protected characteristics in the Act. That means that there are nine groups of people who have their rights protected by the Act – try to name all nine areas. As a start for this task – gender is one.

Answer:
- age
- disability
- gender reassignment
- marriage and civil partnership
- pregnancy and maternity
- race
- religion or belief
- sex (gender)
- sexual orientation.

(based on Acas 2015)

You will see that as well as gender there is sexual orientation and gender reassignment in the list, and all three come into the areas that this book discusses.

In addition to areas of protected characteristics there are also different categories of discrimination that the Act covers.

Direct discrimination

The most obvious and straightforward category is direct discrimination, and this can be (1) to the person who has the protected characteristic, (2) by association or (3) by perception. Discrimination by association is discrimination against someone who has a connection (such as being their friend) with a person who has the protected characteristic, and discrimination by perception is discrimination against someone perceived (or thought of) as having the protected characteristic.

CASE STUDY 2.1:
DISCRIMINATION UNDER THE ACT

Elly has been appointed as a room leader in a baby room. One week after her appointment she discovers that she is pregnant and informs her manager. The next day the manager takes her aside and tells her that they will be giving the post to someone else, as 'You won't be able to lift the babies now that you are expecting.'

REFLECTION

This is an obvious clear case of discrimination against the person who has a protected characteristic. The manager has no way of knowing if Elly will be able to lift the babies or not and has made assumptions and acted in a discriminatory manner. Elly has a case under the Equality Act.

The following case study gives an example of direct discrimination by association: that is, if an employee is a friend with, or supports someone who has a protected characteristic and is treated in a discriminatory way because of it.

CASE STUDY 2.2:
DISCRIMINATION BY ASSOCIATION

Julia is a manager in a nursery that is part of a chain of five nurseries that are privately owned. Her partner is trans and she has spoken openly about this in the staff room. As part of her role she attends regular area gatherings of other managers and once a year the entire staff team from all of the nurseries and their partners and children are invited to the owner's house for a summer barbeque on a weekend day.

This yearly event is a highlight for everyone as there is entertainment and lovely food and drink and it is seen as a summer bonus and a thank you. Prizes and awards are given out and everyone leaves with a gift. Julia receives her invite and notes that it just says her name and not her partner's. When she brings this up at a coffee break at the next area gathering there is silence and no one replies to her or looks at her.

REFLECTION

Julia has a case for discrimination under the Equality Act. Although this is a social event it is work based and seen as a perk that is enjoyed by staff and their families. To exclude Julia's partner is discriminatory towards Julia as everyone else there will have his or her partner (if they have one) with him or her. Julia is also aware that this is an issue that has been discussed without her knowledge.

Finally in this section of the Act, there is also direct discrimination by perception. As a reminder, that is where someone is discriminating against someone because they *think* they have one of the protected characteristics.

CASE STUDY 2.3:
DISCRIMINATION BY PERCEPTION

Rob works in a reception class. He has been there a couple of years and feels that it is time he had some experience with older children. He has a regular supervision session with his manager (and class teacher) and asks her to consider him for a year 6 position that has just come up. She shakes her head and says to him, 'Oh I don't think so.' When he asks her why she says that the other reception teacher, the other assistants and the parents really like him and adds, 'It's the first time we've had someone like you working here and we were a bit worried but it's worked out so well that we don't want to lose you.' While appreciating that his work is valued Rob questions her on 'someone like you'. The teacher looks uncomfortable and says, 'Well, you know, someone gay. We don't want to lose you to all of those rough year 6's. You stay with us – you're so gentle and lovely.'

Rob tells her that he is not gay but she clearly doesn't believe him.

REFLECTION
Apart from all of the assumptions that are being made here about gay men, Rob is being discriminated against because he is perceived as having a protected characteristic.

Other forms of discrimination

There are many ways that discrimination can manifest itself and unfortunately they can all be found in the early years workplace under the umbrella term of 'harassment'. These can include but not be restricted to jokes and gossip that are inappropriate. These can be passed off as 'banter' but can intimidate and isolate an employee if they don't join in and result in them feeling awkward and embarrassed if they do.

The person or people delivering this behaviour can try to pass it off as 'only a joke' but under the Act it is the viewpoint of the person receiving it that's important.

This behaviour can be verbal, written or physical, and can be because the person has a protected characteristic, is linked in some way with someone who has or is perceived to have one or more protected characteristics.

Can you see that the example of Julia in Case Study 2.2 can be harassment as well as direct discrimination?

Note that this can apply to someone who doesn't share the protected characteristic but is uncomfortable with something that is happening at work, for example, someone who hears continual anti-Muslim remarks in the staff room – even though they aren't a Muslim. Or someone who works in a room where there are 'jokes' about people who are trans. All of these remarks, 'jokes' or social chat can have a negative impact on the working environment even if they are wrapped up as 'banter'.

Let's not forget that this book is about children as well as the people who work with them. The Equality Act will also affect children. They look to us, the adults, as a blueprint and positive role model of how to be grown up – how to be 'big'. Being cared for in an environment where someone is unhappy because of discrimination, in whatever form, is going to be detrimental to the children's wellbeing and future emotional and social development as well as the adults'.

Conclusion

A final point about the Equality Act is just to note that, of course, a person can share multiple areas of the protected characteristics. For example, they can be a lesbian who has a disability or someone who has a faith or religion and is also a trans person.

Chapter 3

THE MANAGER

The responsibility and the impetus for good equalities practice must stem from the manager of a setting. I have written in a previous book about the difference between leading and managing (Price and Ota 2104) and here I just need to clarify some key points.

Managing is the day-to-day organisation of a setting. This includes all the routine jobs that have to be completed in order to ensure that the setting runs like clockwork: jobs like managing staff rotas, ordering supplies, collecting money from parents and local authority grants, arranging cover for sickness and organising staff training. The manager makes sure that the arrangements for the smooth functioning of a setting are in place and run like clockwork.

Leading is something different. The role of a leader involves heading up a staff team to deliver the best practice that they can. The leader shows the rest of the team how to be inspiring role models for the children and to work in true partnership with parents. The leader is the person who motivates the team and ensures that they are working towards the mission or vision statement.

The leader also has to ensure that all policies and directives from the local authority and other bodies, for example Ofsted, are complied with and assimilated into the day-to-day running of the setting. In fact this kind of work is split between the manager and leader role. The manager makes sure that there is day-to-day implementation in routines and arrangements. The leader has to think about the spirit of a directive and how that can be captured in the settings practice.

Without an inspiring leader the early years setting is just a business that provides day care to the standards required. The leader thinks about early years and the direction that the setting wants to go in. There should always be an emphasis on considering what is new and exciting in early years – what issues are on the horizon and how the setting can ensure that they are prepared for the future.

Leaders need followers and the leader of an early years setting needs the staff team behind them. This means a staff team that understands and is committed to best practice in equalities. This is very important in terms of thinking about good equalities practice, and especially in terms of gender diversity and sexuality.

When we think of the policies that underpin the settings practice, equalities usually comes quite high up the list. Gender should be part of that. There should be a statement on the equalities policy and/or the vision statement that talks about how we support boys and girls to reach their full potential without stereotyping them. It is the manager's responsibility to ensure that this good practice is put into writing and distributed to staff and parents. The manager/leader/owner of the setting is the person who is ultimately responsible for the setting in terms of Ofsted and it is imperative that they make the equalities practice and policy clear to the staff team and ensure that all members understand the policy and are able to carry it out in practice.

Mission statements

Has your setting got a mission statement? This is a statement of aims and ethos of the setting and can sometimes be known as a vision statement.

When thinking about a vision statement, Kotter (cited in Gill 2006: 98) can help in offering six characteristics of a good vision:

- imaginable
- desirable
- feasible
- focused
- flexible
- communicable: can you explain it in five minutes?

In terms of gender and sexuality it's helpful if the vision statement includes a reference to these, even if it's not at the forefront. For example, 'We aim to provide a caring and happy environment where all children are welcome and encouraged to express themselves, learn, succeed and flourish.' Here you are emphasising that all children are able to express themselves, and this is an indication that you are not going to impose a set of adult-led beliefs and values on children.

ACTIVITY 3.1: WORKING WITH A VISION STATEMENT

Now find the mission or vision statement for your setting. Does it include any statements or references to children being able to express themselves and being supported in that expression? It's a good idea to periodically review the mission statement and make sure that it is up to date with any current policies or legislation. It's also a good idea to check that all staff have seen it and *agree* with it. You may have new staff who joined some time after it was written and who now need to see it and understand that it has to reflect their core values.

REFLECTION

Looking at the mission statement is a really good way of bringing together a group of people who may have very different ideas and views on gender and sexuality, especially in the early years. However, by agreeing with the statement they can all have a consensus on one thing – they are all there to help children grow and flourish and be the truest version of themselves that they can be.

The vision statement is also a good way of reminding parents that this is what the setting stands by and this is what guides its practice.

CASE STUDY 3.1:
MISSION STATEMENTS

A parent comes into the nursery and takes Joyce, the room leader, to one side and asks, 'Is it true that my Billy is dressing up in girls' clothes?' Joyce knows that Billy does enjoy putting on all of the clothes in the dressing-up box and using them in his role-play. 'Yes,' she replies, 'Billy really enjoys trying on all of the clothes that we have and making up stories about them – he's so creative in his use of language.'

The parent is still not happy. 'Well I want you to stop him if he's prancing about in dresses and princess clothes – it's not right.'

Joyce shows the parent their mission statement and reminds them that the setting encourages all children to express themselves in whatever way they choose. She is also very clear that when joining the setting the parent has agreed to the settings policies and procedures and that this vision statement is included in that.

She then takes the parent over to the dressing-up clothes and shows them that the setting prefers not to have branded or gender-specific clothes but rather a selection of clothes and generic pieces that can be adapted and made into whatever the child wants them to be that day.

REFLECTION

Have you had a situation like that at your setting?

How would you deal with it?

Can you see how being able to refer the parent to the vision statement is a useful tool?

I think that this is especially useful when a member of staff is new or not very confident at challenging parents or defending the setting's position. It makes things much less personal and helps by establishing a starting point that supporting a child's wishes in terms of gender is part of a wider picture of enabling a child to be whoever they want to be in all aspects of their young lives so that they can be nurtured into adulthood.

CASE STUDY 3.2: BOOKS FOR BOYS AND BOOKS FOR GIRLS

Maria is the manager of a large day nursery. There is a new staff member in the three–five-year room and Maria has made some time in the afternoon to come into the room informally in order to observe the new practitioner.

She overhears the practitioner talking to some children (boys) in the book corner.

'Well that's a lovely book, let's have a look at it together, there's a princess on it. Are you sure that you want this one? I have another one here that has dinosaurs and monsters in it. You'd probably prefer that one, wouldn't you?'

What do you think Maria could say to the staff member?

REFLECTION
First, I would advise not going straight in and reprimanding the staff member in front of the rest of the room team and the children. It is always wise to choose a time and a place where people can talk more honestly without the pressures of time or other people watching.

I would also ask you to notice that I haven't specified the gender of the practitioner and I can reveal now that his name is Ben. Does that change your reaction at all? Perhaps you think that Ben would have a 'right' to make these kind of observations as he is a man. It might be that a practitioner would find it harder to challenge Ben as they might feel that he is entitled to hold these views. It is useful to think about how the gender of a practitioner can change the way that you would think about this situation, but the situation itself remains the same.

The reason I have written this case study in this section is that I think that policies and vision statements are a useful tool to use when there is a situation of differing values. It can make the situation less personal and fraught.

Maria can remind Ben that during his first few days in the setting he was given a range of policies, including an equalities policy, and that he had signed to say that he had read them. In the policy it is stated that boys and girls should be able to freely access all toys and resources and that staff members should support their choices. Maria can ask Ben about the conversation and encourage him to reflect on how this recent incident doesn't move his practice towards the policy but away from it.

She could have a general discussion about how this policy could be interpreted and if Ben is happy and comfortable with this kind of practice. Afterwards she might talk to her management team and think of how new staff in the future could have a fuller induction to the equalities policies, and how the next staff meeting could be given over to thinking about gender generally and the way that we talk to and treat boys and girls. In this discussion it would be useful to think about and reflect on everyone's upbringing. Did they think that they were presented with a stereotypical way to be a man or a woman when they were growing up? Did they feel any pressure to conform and 'not be a cissy' or to be a 'pretty girl'? Some of these ideas could be so entrenched in someone's personality that it can be hard to identify them and see how they can affect the practice in the setting.

The manager needs to be aware of the role models that the staff team are showing to children in terms of attitudes towards gender and should feel confident enough to challenge and hold them accountable if they are not meeting the sentiments of the mission statement. The manager should also be able to support staff if they have to defend the settings position to a parent or carer or other outside person.

Finally I wish to look at Ofsted and how the manager can use this good practice in gender to meet statutory requirements.

Ofsted

As well as the mission statement there are statements from Ofsted that cover equalities in the wellbeing section of the Inspection Handbook, such as 'The effectiveness of care practices in helping children feel emotionally secure and ensuring that children are physically and emotionally healthy' (Ofsted 2015: 36).

The Early Years Foundation Stage (EYFS) has four underpinning statements and central to them all is the overarching responsibility that the setting has towards the children that they care for. This responsibility has to be guided by the current legislative directives that direct practitioners and settings in matters of welfare and education.

Indeed the EYFS is referred to in the most recent childcare legislation – the Children and Families Act 2014. Equality of opportunity and anti-discriminatory practice, ensuring that every child is included and supported. (Department for Education 2014: 5)

The EYFS and its non-statutory accompaniment 'Development Matters' do not specifically mention gender or providing an environment that is supportive to young children exploring gender roles. However, many of the statements that are made have this sensitive understanding as an unspoken prerequisite for many of the requirements. For example, the following statement comes from the section in 'Development Matters' on 'making relationships' regarding how adults could encourage children between

30 and 50 months in this: 'Support children in developing positive relationships by challenging negative comments and actions towards either peers or adults' (Early Education 2012: 9). I think that encouraging children to talk freely about gender roles in a positive way and providing positive role models and an enabling environment would be part of this adult-led task.

The responsibility of providers to ensure that they are supporting children with positive discussions and role models about gender and providing an enabling environment that helps this process is not specifically commented on in the Ofsted framework, as I have already noted it is not in the EYFS. However, as with the EYFS, there are some overarching statements that I feel can be underpinned by the work that I am suggesting here. For example, in the Inspector's Handbook (Ofsted 2015), an outstanding provision has this said about it: 'The extremely sharp focus on helping them to acquire communication and language skills, and on supporting their physical, personal, social and emotional development helps all children make rapid improvement in their learning from their starting points' (Ofsted 2015: 34).

I feel that if children are being supported in having open discussions about gender and the choices that they are making then it feeds into their healthy emotional development. A practical example of this would be the little boy who is able to play with dolls and dressing-up clothes without being steered away from them as not being gender suitable for him. I refer to incidents like this many times in other chapters.

I also draw your attention to the wellbeing section which states that inspectors must assess 'The effectiveness of care practices in helping children feel emotionally secure and ensuring that children are physically and emotionally healthy' (Ofsted 2015: 36). Again, I believe that an enabling environment that supports the choices that children make without stereotyping is part of the work that is needed in order to help children feel good about themselves.

An outstanding provision in terms of wellbeing meets the following criteria:

Care practices are better than good because:

- All practitioners are highly skilled and sensitive in helping children of all ages form secure emotional attachments, and provide a strong base for helping them in developing their independence and ability to explore.
- Children increasingly show high levels of self-control during activities and confidence in social situations, and are developing an excellent understanding of how to manage risks and challenges relative to their age.
- Children's safety and safeguarding is central to everything all practitioners do. They effectively support children's growing understanding of how to keep themselves safe and healthy.
- There is a highly stimulating environment with child-accessible resources that promote learning and challenge children both in and outdoors.

The strong skills of all key persons ensure all children are emotionally well prepared for the next stages in their learning. Practitioners skillfully support children's transitions both within the setting and to other settings and school (Tayler and Price 2016: 33).

Conclusion

It is important that the manager is a leader of inspiring and forward-thinking good practice as well as a manager of the day-to-day routines. In order to do this there will have to be some full and frank discussions in the staff room about gender and sexuality and the moral compass of the people who are working in the setting and caring and educating the children who attend. This also affects how they are working with the families of those children and is crucial to practice.

I would suggest that a manager ensures that communication systems in the setting and within the staff team are conducive to such sensitive discussions so that there can be a consensus within the staff team on how to reflect positive gender practice and avoid stereotyping and assumptions.

I give some additional suggestions for training in other chapters.

Chapter 4

THE TEAM AND THE INDIVIDUAL PRACTITIONER IN THE SETTING

In this chapter I am going to look at some ideas for activities in the setting and also give an outline for ideas for team training sessions. This chapter is also linked to the chapters on resources and the environment – Chapters 5 and 6 – as there are ideas for practice in those chapters as well.

Grouping children

Generally when getting children into groups it is better practice to avoid dividing them by gender. Another thing that practitioners sometimes do is to ask children to choose a friend. This can also be problematic for children. They might have more than one friend and be worrying about hurting someone's feelings or they might not have a particular friend. In terms of gender they might want to choose a boy or a girl but be worried about their reaction and the reaction of their peer group. There are so many different ways to group children and the activity of grouping them can be creative in itself.

ACTIVITY 4.1: WAYS OF GROUPING CHILDREN

Ask children to find someone else who likes the same colour as them, or has the same pet as them or the same thing for breakfast; ask them to find someone who has the same size feet or hands as them, or the same colour eyes or hair.

Another idea is to get the children to choose an animal and try to look like that animal, and then find another child who is being the same animal. This is a simple activity, full of conversation and also social and physical skills.

You could also make some cards: pictures that have been divided into three or four pieces depending on what size groups you want. Each child is given a piece of one of the pictures, and then tries to find the other parts of the picture. Animals are good for this activity as they are recognisable and simple. There are commercial versions of these cards, or they can be customised to the setting and children's interests and laminated.

Persona Dolls

Many of the activities that are good practice in terms of gender and sexuality are about the resources in the setting and specific attitudes of the practitioners rather than tailor-made activities. However, Persona Dolls are an interesting resource for exploring gender and sexuality with children.

Persona Dolls are large child-sized dolls that are not toys. They are members of the setting and have a personality and character that is created for them. This can sound a bit 'creepy' to some people but children accept Persona Dolls very well and they can be a sensitive and creative way to discuss 'issues' and link them to a childlike being that children already know and like. The Persona Doll Training website (personadoll.uk) gives a good overview of how to use the dolls and how to manage them in the setting and get the best use of them. They can often be borrowed from resource libraries. The training to use the dolls is important as they are a big purchase and need to be used thoughtfully; they cannot be left in the home corner as a toy, and to just buy them and keep them on a shelf as staff are unsure or not confident in their use is a waste of resources.

CASE STUDY 4.1: USING A PERSONA DOLL

Jodie, a practitioner in a nursery, has worked hard to establish Jay, the Persona Doll, with the children. She has introduced Jay to the group as a visitor and given them a background story. Jay is four and lives at home with their mum and dad and has a sister who is nine years old. Jay likes to look at books and play games with friends, and especially enjoys drawing and painting.

One day Jodie gathers the children together and sits Jay on her knee. 'Today Jay wants to talk to you about a problem. Everyone who knows Jay thinks that Jay is a boy but Jay wants to grow their hair longer and wants to wear dresses, not just at dressing-up time at nursery but all the time. Jay wants people to say "she" when they are talking about her. Some of the children at the nursery that Jay goes to have been horrible to her and said that she shouldn't wear dresses because she's a boy. Jay feels very sad. What do we think?'

REFLECTION

Whatever answers the children give, this is an interesting scenario for them to consider. It is important that this isn't the first time that they have met Jay and that they have a relationship with and knowledge of Jay before this is introduced as an issue. In that way they are more likely to want to show concern and empathy for Jay's predicament and to think sympathetically about a solution.

Jodie has been careful in introducing Jay not to use male pronouns very much, and to make Jay's interests non-stereotypically specific.

It might be that none of the children in that class will be exploring their gender or sexuality as they grow older. In a way that doesn't matter. It is equally important that children are aware that there may be other children who are going through this process and that they are supportive and sympathetic to them. We want to support children who are going through this process. Equally we want to support children who are outside this process so that they can feel understanding and exhibit reassurance to their peers.

Staff training

The most important and valuable resource that a setting has is its staff team. I was an Ofsted and local government inspector and saw many early years settings during my career. I have seen excellent and respectful practice being carried out in settings where the resources are limited and money is tight, and indifferent practice in state-of-the art purpose-built settings where no expense has been spared.

Central to this is staff training. I have written about leading and managing and the problems with training in early years settings in Tayler and Price (2016). Here I just want to note that I am aware of the issues that can restrict its availability:

- staff having to attend meetings and training in their own time
- local authorities charging for training that used to be free
- settings prioritising their training budget in order to fund qualification training, perhaps so that staff can be counted in higher staff:child ratios
- no suitable place for the whole staff team to gather.

It's impossible to address many of these issues in this book. However, I would say that if funding is an issue then it could be useful to get together with other local settings and hire a trainer. For the purposes of this book Stonewall have a team of excellent trainers for thinking about gender diversity and sexuality.

Also, below I have made some suggestions for in-house staff training, although I would always stress that it is best to use a specialist in the field.

ACTIVITY 4.2:
ONE-HOUR TRAINING

Ask the team to pair with someone they don't know very well. Give each couple two copies of a list of questions that they have to answer about their partner *without* asking them the answer. Examples of questions are:

- What is this person's favourite food?
- What music do they like?
- Where, ideally, would they like to go on holiday?
- Who was their teenage heartthrob?
- What would they drink on a night out?
- What colour is their favourite?

About ten questions is the right length. If people ask how they are to do this then the answer is to guess or to look at them. It should be done in silence and when the couple have finished the activity they should exchange answers.

REFLECTION

This is a fun activity and certainly is valuable as a general team-building resource as people get to know more about each other and discover differences and similarities. However, the real worth of this is the process. Ask the team how they reached the conclusions they reached. The answer generally is that they made assumptions based on what their partner looks like, the image they project, their age, gender, what the person likes themselves, and sometimes they give 'safe' answers that they think no one could take offence at.

The point is that the answers are not based on the reality of the situation as the participants couldn't ask their partner. In this case it doesn't matter. However, if they are working with children and families and acting on information that they haven't checked out to be true then there could be a problem: 'Oh, he won't want to do that because he's a boy,' or 'They put strange food in their lunch box, that could be neglect.' As practitioners, if we are thinking something about a child and/or a family we should always check it out to see if it's a real thought based on fact or one that's based on an assumption that has come from a cocktail of our own backgrounds and experiences, influences from the media, and so on.

ACTIVITY 4.3: HALF-DAY TRAINING

As a warm-up, ask staff to line up in order of the first initial of their middle name and then talk about how they got that name. We sometimes have interesting stories about these and it's a useful ice breaker.

I would then suggest starting with Activity 4.2 above, followed by a break.

After this, ask staff in pairs to reflect on assumptions they make about men and women. Ask them to list under the headings 'What is a man?' and 'What is a woman?' what characteristics each have (for example, 'caring' under the heading 'What is a woman?' and 'tough' under the heading 'What is a man?'). Then the pairs get into groups of four and discuss whether there are any characteristics listed they completely agree with or disagree with.

As a follow-up ask staff to suggest activities that are for boys and then some for girls.

REFLECTION

These conversations will allow staff members to come to a realisation that there are very few – if any – definite characteristics (rather than physical attributes) that make up masculinity or femininity.

In fact we are all on a sliding scale and our position on it keeps moving throughout our lives. When I was a child I was very characteristically and stereotypically feminine with dolls and frills. When I was older I took on a physically demanding job that was a contradiction to that. But I was the same person all through.

When discussing activities I am sure that staff will also realise that all activities are for all children. It just depends on their interests and preferences. We could also discuss how much these interests and preferences are manipulated by parents and media influences. If possible during this discussion look at the website Let Toys be Toys (http://lettoysbetoys.org.uk) for examples and ideas around resources that are not gender specific.

ACTIVITY 4.4:
WHOLE-DAY TRAINING

Start the day with Activity 4.3.

After a lunch break show the video *Redraw the Balance* on the website of MullenLowe Group (www.youtube.com/watch?v=qv8VZVP5csA).

Discuss afterwards how the setting could improve the activities and resources it offers to ensure that children get a positive view of men and women and what their roles are.

Look at Stonewall's pack *Getting Started: A Toolkit for Preventing and Tackling Homophobic, Biphobic and Transphobic Bullying in Primary Schools* (2016; www.stonewall.org.uk/sites/default/files/getting_started_toolkit_-_primary.pdf). Print off the glossary and the child-friendly explanations and as a team discuss how comfortable you are with these.

End by asking all participants to think of one way that they can move their practice forward.

Conclusion

I hope that this chapter has given some useful ideas of how to move practice forward in the setting. I think that it's important to move people on from where they are and this can only happen with open and full discussions as a staff team. Underpinning this, there has to be a feeling of trust within the team. If this is lacking then establishing and addressing this is a priority, before following the activities suggested in this chapter, as without it the staff training sessions will be tokenistic at best and meet with resistance and entrenchment at worst.

Chapter 5

THE ENVIRONMENT OF THE SETTING AND IDEAS FOR ACTIVITIES

Start as you mean to go on

ACTIVITY 5.1: EQUALITIES AUDIT

I suggest a daily 'equalities check' on the play and learning environment. When doing this in its entirety the practitioner might find it helpful to consider the following:

- What do the children see when they look at their environment?

- Is there anything that reinforces any gender stereotypes they may already have absorbed?
- What is neutral?
- What challenges, interests, extends, develops and/or offers opportunities for questions and discussion?

The walls of the setting

As part of this audit look specifically at the walls of the setting. This is the area that is most looked at by children and parents and carers. Traditionally early years settings have always had bright, eye-catching images on the walls. I would suggest that these are initiated, inspired and contributed to by the children and their families in order to make them meaningful and for the children and their families to feel included and that they have a voice.

It has been mentioned elsewhere in this book but it cannot be overemphasised how important it is for families and children to have their lives reflected back at them. In this way the setting validates their lives and it all contributes to the setting having a feeling of community, which is essential if children are going to learn, grow and thrive in this environment. This is important throughout the range of equalities issues, and nowhere more so than with gender. As well as reflecting the lives of the children and families who use the setting, there is also an opportunity to extend understanding by including the lives of families the users may be unfamiliar with. This is especially important in areas where there is not much diversity.

As an Ofsted inspector I often saw beautiful, artistic displays in a setting and in discussion I found out that these had been created by practitioners from their own interests and starting points. In an ideal world the practitioners themselves should reflect the children and families in terms of gender, culture and class. This is not always possible, and certainly most settings are in the position of having a mainly female workforce who are caring for and educating boys. If the practitioners do not reflect the families and children that they care for then they certainly need to ensure that the visual environment that the children are in does.

ACTIVITY 5.2: LOOKING AT DISPLAYS

- If the visual environment on the walls is intended for the children is it at the right height for them to be able to look at it easily?
- How often is it changed?
- What does it reflect?
- Have the children made an input to it?
- Do any headings or other written matter draw parents to look/think/ask questions?

ACTIVITY 5.3: PHOTO DISPLAY

If you would like to start a new display then this would be a great activity to do, and is so much easier now with the use of digital cameras and cheap and easy access to printing.

Take lots of photos of the current group(s) of children doing things that they enjoy and ensure there are plenty of children engaged in non-stereotypical activities, such as girls and boys building together, boys and girls dressing up together, girls running, playing football, climbing, boys washing up, watering plants, cooking. It is important that the children see the photos, talk about them and agree which ones to put up, and where possible, there should also be paintings and drawings alongside them selected by the children themselves.

This homemade display could be enhanced by carefully vetted published material like Stonewall posters (available at www.stonewall.org.uk) showing different family structures. In addition there could be words and photos for parents with ideas of activities to do at home around 'celebrating difference' and different families.

This is quite a general resource for promoting diversity but thinking about gender specifically, it could focus on experiencing and understanding feelings which could counter 'boys don't cry' and 'girls aren't loud/angry/ boisterous', for example.

Other areas of the setting

The toilet and coats areas

As well as the general wall space in the setting the area that parents and carers and their children will see first when they enter the setting is the coats area and after that probably the toilet area. With this in mind I suggest:

- Don't separate girls' and boys' toilets if at all possible.
- Have mixed coat peg areas.
- If there are peg pictures or colours make sure they are not all 'pretty flowers' and pastel shades for the girls and 'wild animals' and bright colours for the boys! Have a wide range of images and good strong colours, and let the children choose.

Role-play area: general ideas for a diverse and welcoming area

- Make it as 'real' as possible and try to reflect the children's homes. For example, bowls and chopsticks should be included if there are Chinese children in the group.
- Include tools, large paintbrushes, a tray or box of earth or sand and small trowels, old seed packets. Include old clocks, radios, computer keyboard and

screwdrivers and pliers so that boys and girls can do 'fixing'. This takes the role-play area out of the sphere of traditionally female domestic tasks.

• Have the role-play area next to the large block area so that 'extensions'/building work can take place.

• Include buckets, trowels, and so on in the block area. Have a mark-making area close to the role-play area too so that menus, building plans, lists and so on can be made.

CASE STUDY 5.1:
WHO USES A TOOLBOX?

A story I would like to share is that of a friend who was a single parent. Her daughter had only ever seen her mother do small jobs around the house. She had seen her put up shelves, garden, change light bulbs, decorate and fix electrical equipment. When her daughter started preschool she came back one day, pointed to the picture in a book of a toolbox, and said, 'That's for the daddies.'

REFLECTION
How do you feel when you read this? Do you think, 'Well that's the way it is, mostly the tools are for the daddies,' or 'She may have got that idea from the TV, not from the preschool'? You might be thinking about your setting and wondering if

there is some way that you could be countering the overwhelming messages about gender that my friend's daughter will be getting from the other influences in her life. These messages are strong enough to contradict the actual reality of that child's life.

Dressing-up area

- The dressing-up area should include clothes that are realistic and good quality, rather than just fairy and 'Frozen' dresses at one end of the rail and superhero outfits at the other.
- There should be a wide range of appropriately sized trousers, skirts, jackets, child-size sari lengths, tops, wings, hats, scarves and boxes of bags, including small suitcases/rucksacks, first aid and lunch boxes, handbags, shoulder bags and purses.
- Also, include plenty of opportunities to be creative – lengths of material, belts, ties, scarves, with support from adults with scissors, sewing and tying as necessary. It is good to have both large and small mirrors too.

Book area

- Make the area comfortable and inviting, maybe with a sofa to sprawl on as well as lots of cushions and rugs.

- Here too it is good to have photos of current children, boys and girls, reading or perhaps acting out a story and again, changed regularly.
- Provide a wide range of easily accessible books, including plenty with girls taking the lead role and which challenge gender stereotypes.
- Include books with boys showing caring behaviour and enjoying traditionally 'girly' activities.
- There should be books with a wide variety of family make-up to include same-sex parents. Make sure this is not tokenistic, for example one book with a boy in a dress and one with a girl playing football!
- Make books with the children with photos of them doing non-stereotypical activities they enjoy and have these books available in the book corner.
- If possible have a parents' book corner in the same room so they can both look at their children's books and browse/borrow for themselves.
- Make sure there is an up-to-date selection of attractive books that cover all the issues of transgender and gender-creative children and all aspects of gender stereotyping, and make sure these books are visible and easily accessible.

There's more about where to access these kinds of resources in Chapter 9. I would also add that it is important to regularly audit these areas, especially the book corner. Make sure that books are attractive and in good condition and move them around so that the most accessible books change regularly.

Outdoor play

- 'Real' activities should be available as much as possible: mud play, digging, planting, weeding, picking, sand and water.
- Replicate and extend indoor role-play so that the outside is valued as much as the inside. Some ideas to include are ball games, climbing, tents, dens, building sites, shops, and so on.
- Ensure that it is not just the male staff who are outside with the children, and that all staff are seen to value and enjoy outdoor play – whatever the weather!

General discussion about the teaching and learning environment

- Support all children to take part in all the above play and learning activities.
- The way the areas have been set up and the materials provided already help to break down the usual stereotypes.
- Talk about choosing and why we choose certain things.
- Talk about who does what and why.
- Show that reasons are actually rarely to do with gender but more to do with 'fitting in'/doing what's expected of us. Challenge this with the children.
- Think about your language and your own attitudes – this has been discussed further in Chapter 4 on the

staff team, but is worth mentioning here in terms of the way that the staff react to the environment.

- Think about referring to children as people, not boys and girls.
- Praise the act not the person: 'Wow, you made a great building there,' rather than 'Aren't you a good girl.'
- Refer to people by name, which makes any comment specific to that child. Remember, who we are changes with how we feel/what we're doing.
- Using a Persona Doll to talk about issues with the children is a wonderful way of drawing them into discussion and highlighting any concerns and/or lack of understanding (see more about this resource in Chapter 9). In terms of gender, you could think about using the doll to talk about 'I like to dress up in the blue dress and hat but Jane says boys can't' or 'George won't let me play football with the boys 'cos he says girls can't play.'

Involving parents and carers and using them as part of the environment and resources of the setting

- Invite a father with a baby to come in and bath and change the baby with the children; follow up with bathing, dressing and feeding activities with the boys and girls with the dolls.

- Invite a woman firefighter to show equipment and talk about what she does in her role; follow up with making/painting a fire engine from boxes, dressing up and putting out fires with the girls and the boys.

ACTIVITY 5.4: GROWING UP

Watch MullenLowe Group's video *Redraw the Balance* (www.youtube.com/watch?v=qv8VZVP5csA; also featured in Activity 4.4), which details how children in early years already define career opportunities as either male or female.

REFLECTION
How did you feel after this? Were you surprised at the children's reactions? Pleased that the women were such positive role models for the children but sad that they were not reflected in the children's perceptions of those roles?

Conclusion

This chapter has outlined a range of ways that you can audit and reflect on the environment that you provide for children and their families. We have looked specifically at gender but inevitably there are some ideas there that will ensure that other areas of diversity will also be covered. This is an ongoing process and it's important that it's not a one-off activity. As the first activity makes clear, it's as important to do an equalities check as it is to do a health and safety check for your setting. This chapter needs to be read in conjunction with Chapter 9, on resources, so that you know what to do and where to access materials in order to move forward and create a welcoming and positive early years environment.

Chapter 6

SUPPORTING FAMILIES

This chapter will discuss ways to work with the families of the children that you care for in the early years setting. We are focusing on gender issues but of course there are many other ways that you will be supporting families and this chapter is by no means exhaustive as we are just focusing on two areas of your support role.

Underpinning all of the work that you do with families is your relationships with each other. It's so important to have a close, professional and respectful relationship with the families of the children you care for and this is especially important when thinking about gender and sexuality, as they can be such sensitive issues.

CASE STUDY 6.1: BOYS' ACTIVITIES

Jessica works in a preschool. One of her key children is Aaron who is nearly four years old. Aaron has always been fond of art activities and especially likes gluing and sticking. He can spend all of the session working on intricate mosaics or collages. His mother, Lucy, has always been pleased with his art works and has shared with Jessica some of the pieces that Aaron has made at home.

More recently Jessica has noticed that Lucy seems irritated when she comes to pick Aaron up and finds him working on his projects. 'For heaven's sake Aaron,' she said the other day, 'Go out and get some fresh air and kick a ball about like a real boy.' She saw Jessica looking at her and shook her head. 'I know that I shouldn't do this but I'm worried that when he gets to school he'll have no friends because he doesn't do the things that other boys do.'

What would you say to Lucy?

REFLECTION

There are many things you could say but they all rely on your relationship with Lucy and how much she trusts your judgement. I always think that it helps to start where the person is rather than come in and try to get them to see your point of view immediately. Lucy knows that it is not 'right' to try to get Aaron to behave differently and so might be very defensive if challenged. There is also a point of view that it would be good for Aaron to get some physical exercise along with all of the children and that could be addressed as a whole-group thing rather than singling Aaron out.

Jessica might be able to address Lucy's fears about Aaron's friendship group at school and also dig deeper to see if Lucy is worried about Aaron in other ways. She might think that wanting to do art and craft activities means that Aaron is gay. He may or may not be, and that is something Lucy might be able to discuss with Jessica if they have a close and trusting relationship.

Initial contact

The first contact that is made with a parent/carer is very important in establishing the respectful relationship that is to follow. Many settings use an 'All about me' type form that the parent completes and brings into the setting and that has general information about them and the child.

This is the crucial moment when it is important to establish that the setting is welcoming and inclusive. When searching for examples of such forms online I saw many that had 'Mother' and 'Father' headings. What about the single parent or same-sex parent? How would it feel as a parent handing in a form with a blank space? Would they feel the need to apologise for not conforming to the nursery's idea of what a 'family' should be? As part of this discussion a parent in a same-sex relationship recently said to me, 'I'm so sick of people asking me or my daughter who her "real" mother is. How dare they make assumptions about the biological mother and the validity of her relationship with our daughter as compared to the other "less real" mother?' Have a think about this statement and how your setting might view this.

This form should be the start of the close and trusting relationship that is built between the setting and the parent. There should be a shared understanding that the key worker is aware of the tremendous leap of trust that the parent is making in leaving their child in the setting's care. In return the practitioner needs to understand that their side of the contract that is being established is to value the parent and to try to provide a consistent level of care in terms of valuing the home and family life that the child is rooted in.

The setting and the parent have an interdependent relationship where they both need each other. The child should also have agency in this relationship so as to maximise the likelihood of there being a continuity of care and education as adults and children would be clear as to what that consists of.

Seen in this way the key worker should make good use of the initial form to find out as much detail about the family as they can. It is important to make sure that they pronounce the child's and the parent's names correctly and don't use an abbreviation without checking first if that's OK. I've lost count of the many times I'm called 'Debbie' when it's something I especially hate!

There is a whole chapter (Chapter 7) in this book that discusses the special support we can give a parent in terms of a child who is exploring their gender identity. This chapter is just about supporting parents generally. Part of that support is to make the parent aware of the setting's policy concerning gender and ensuring that children can be who they want to be and play with whatever toys and resources they choose.

Initial activities

In the initial settling-in sessions you might want to reassure the parent and the child that their choices are not limited by gender stereotyping.

- You might want to show the parent a range of books that are positive about exploring gender roles – see the book list in Chapter 9.
- You might want to ensure that there are a range of activities that are offered to the child and that assumptions are not made about what might engage or distract them, such as saying, 'Look at this lovely doll' to a girl and 'Shall we go and see what's outside?' to a boy. Instead practitioners might just say, 'What do you like playing with?' as a more open-ended question that would provoke discussion.

- You might make sure that when you are talking to the parent you are not making assumptions about their background, such as if they're with a partner and what gender the partner is, if they work and what kind of job they do, where their ethnic and/or cultural roots are. There are a range of assumptions that we might make about new people that we meet. Many of those can be based around gender and sexuality, for example thinking that it is unusual for a father to want to take on caring responsibilities (see Case Study 6.2 below).

- A pet hate of mine – try to use the parent's name rather than just saying 'Mum' or 'Dad' when talking to them, and if you are talking to the child, don't say, 'Here's Dad,' as though that is their actual name, but say instead, 'Look, here's your dad coming to pick you up.'

CASE STUDY 6.2:
RELATING TO PARENTS

Allie is a room leader in a baby room. She overhears Nikki, a newly qualified assistant, talking to a father, Joe, who has brought his six-month baby in for a settling-in session. They are discussing maternity and paternity leave.

'Oh, you are good bringing in little Sandi,' says Nikki. 'My other half didn't know one end of a nappy from another and was completely hopeless. Sandi's mum is lucky to have you around to do all of this for her.'

Allie isn't sure what to do. She is glad that Nikki has a warm relationship with Joe, as the initial settling-in period can be stressful for both the parent and the child. On the other hand she feels that with her comments Nikki is suggesting that:

- by showing routine caring skills with his daughter Joe is being unlike most fathers and that this is exceptional
- the baby's mother should feel grateful that Joe is fulfilling some of the domestic duties that come with being a parent which Nikki is automatically assigning to the mother.

Apart from this stereotyping Nikki is sharing a level of personal information that is bordering on inappropriate.

What advice would you give Allie?

REFLECTION
However Allie deals with this situation, the important thing is that it needs to be dealt with. I would suggest perhaps starting with the inappropriate information as that is the easiest to clear up: Nikki can just be given the information that she needs to guard against this as it can be

seen as being unprofessional and can also make parents uncomfortable.

Allie needs to explain to Nikki that we need to keep our work professional and child-focused. Chatting should therefore be about the child, not her own or anyone else's family dynamics.

Dealing with the other part of the issue is more about a change of attitude and this cannot be achieved overnight. Remember that I would always advise starting where the person is and leading them on from there. Allie can set up a room meeting where they review the toys, books and resources in the room and talk about the importance of seeing men in a caring role. As part of this training Allie can encourage the staff team to discuss their feelings about this and find out if they have any experience of this or if it's a new thing for them to think about. If it is new then Allie can discuss how important it is for children to see their mothers, fathers and any carers take an equal role in caring for them.

Conclusion

When we are thinking about supporting families in terms of gender and sexuality it is crucial to set the right tone by putting a lot of thought and reflective deliberation into the initial experience of the family when they enter into the contract with the setting. It is key to remember that the family have chosen your setting as the place where they want their child to have care and education while they are elsewhere. It is a privilege that they have given you and you need to respect that.

There are many reasons why this initial contact is so important. It is part of the 'settling in' process and parents and children need to have warm trusting relationships with the setting in order for the child and the carers to feel comfortable. For deep learning and development to happen the child must feel comfortable in the setting and not experience any stress at being left there.

One of the ways that we can think about it is how we want a child and a family to be able to move freely and easily between their home and the setting. It is much more difficult for the child and their family to have to make two jumps – from their home into the home that you represent in the setting through your initial contact forms, your actions and your resources, and then also into the very concept of being away from home and in a care and education setting. Not reflecting the families' home back at them in terms of gender diversity and sexuality is asking them to work twice as hard when settling in and getting used to the setting.

Chapter 7

LGB AND TRANSGENDER ISSUES IN EARLY YEARS

This chapter is dedicated to the memory of Finnian Lytle.

In 2016, 2796 children called Childline seeking help with their gender identity, which equates to eight calls a day (Lyons 2016). The figures that Childline have, as a confidential service, don't allow for the same caller ringing multiple times and they can't be specific as to age but they think that the youngest caller was 11, and they are mainly in the 12–15 age range.

The same article noted that referrals to the Tavistock clinic, which is one of the main centres for children and adolescents and gender issues in England, doubled from 697 in 2014–15 to 1398 in 2015–16. There was also a twofold increase in referrals of children and adolescents to the

Sandyford clinic in Glasgow, from 90 in 2014 to 178 in 2015 (Lyons 2016).

As early years workers does this mean that we can shrug our shoulders and think that these young people aren't in 'our' age range and so are not our concern? Of course not – as early years workers we are not only caring for and educating the child in front of us, but also the young person and adult that they will become so it is very much our concern that children and young people are struggling in this way and not finding support in their immediate surroundings.

Peter Wanless, the chief executive of the NSPCC, said:

> We cannot call ourselves a modern society if we stigmatise children just because they feel different. It is vital that children have support otherwise, as they tell us all too often, they suffer. When a child is made to feel ashamed about who they are, it can trigger serious mental health issues and crippling shame. (Lyons 2016)

There are some shocking statistics about suicide that relate specifically to the young trans community:

> A survey found that 48% of trans people under 26 said they had attempted suicide, and 30% said they had done so in the past year, while 59% said they had at least considered doing so.

> By comparison, about 6% of all 16- to 24-year-olds say they have attempted suicide, according to the Adult Psychiatry Morbidity Survey. (Strudwick 2014)

This last figure is shocking. It is not up to date so we can assume that the actual figure in 2017 may be much higher. We also have to consider whether it would make any difference to those figures if the young people involved had received support and validity when they were much younger. In order to continue as early years practitioners we have to believe that it would. I believe that excellent practice in early years settings does set a template for the child as to how they should be treated, what respectful engagement should look like. Even if this isn't mirrored at home or continued in their later school career, it is a period of safe time where their gender choices were supported.

I want to remind you again that talking about sexuality isn't talking about sex, and that we need to be aware of this investment in the future that we are part of. Many of the gender-positive activities and actions that I have already discussed will also feed into this section. Children who are being cared for and educated in an environment where their choices in terms of gender are respected and supported will feel positive about themselves.

CASE STUDY 7.1: EARLY EXPERIENCES OF BEING TRANS

Robin is a teenager at university who is trans and looks back at their experiences in primary school and nursery.

'I found it very difficult when I started nursery, as at home I had two brothers and just joined in their games with them, no one in my family thought that was unusual at all. Suddenly at nursery I was being told off if I started playing my usual rough and tumble games, especially with the other girls.

It was assumed by the staff that I would always prefer not to go outside if it was wet or muddy and that I would like to sit "nicely" and play with glitter and glue like most of the other girls. There didn't seem to be any attempt to find out what we individually liked, as I know some of the boys would have preferred to do the craft activities rather than get wet and dirty like me, and I'm sure some of the girls would have liked more physical play.

I resisted all efforts to dress me up in the "girly" dressing up clothes and I actually remember hearing one of the staff members say to her colleague "She'd be a pretty little thing if she just made the effort." I felt that there wasn't anyone else like me and didn't know what was wrong with me.

It just got worse as I got older. I didn't want to grow my hair long, put clips in it or wear dresses. At primary school playtime I had no interest in playing with the girls and the boys just laughed at me when I tried to join in with them. That meant that I spent a lot of time on my

own and I know that the teachers thought that
I was deliberately being anti-social and difficult.
The more time I spent away from the other
children the worse the bullying became – it was a
vicious circle.'

REFLECTION
How do you feel when you read this? Is there
anything the nursery could have done to support
Robin in those early years?

Robin and other people like him didn't just wake up one
morning and decide to be trans. People who are trans,
when interviewed, often reflect on always feeling different
and always identifying differently from the sex they were
born into.

There is also some interesting material on the NHS
website (NHS Choices n.d.) that might give you some
medical and biological insights.

It's also important to note that just because someone
identifies as trans, it doesn't also mean that they are lesbian
or gay. The sexuality of a person who is trans is a separate
issue and they may identify as straight, lesbian, gay, bi or
asexual, and this may change after they have had medical
treatment.

At any age, a person should be accepted as trans
regardless of whether there has been medical intervention.
Accepting them could just involve calling them by a

different name and pronoun, and supporting them with some changes in the way that they look, such as the clothes that they wear and the length of their hair.

It's also important to remember that this may or may not change. Preschool children are exploring their gender and what it means to be a boy or a girl, and this might involve exploration of their biological sex and gender identity or the one that they weren't born with. Some children may be uncomfortable with certain gender roles because they are transgender while others may be uncomfortable simply because they want to behave non-stereotypically but remain the gender they were assigned at birth. Neither option is worse or better, and staff should avoid making judgements or jumping to quick assumptions. They are there to support the child in any exploration and in a variety of choices.

For those of us who have always had a comfortable match between the biological gender assigned to us at birth and the gender we feel ourselves to be it can be perplexing to consider how it might feel if this wasn't the case. Many people feel a mismatch, a constant feeling of being in the wrong body, which is called gender dysphoria. It is not a mental illness; it is a recognised medical condition.

Of course, people who are trans, like any other people, may have mental health issues and these may be compounded by years of feeling this dysphoria, and being bullied, humiliated and rejected in their pursuit of feeling 'normal', of striving to have a happy, fulfilled life. This whole journey can begin very early and it is important that, as early years workers, we strive to support all of the children we care for and educate and validate their choices.

Staff and parents and carers

We also need to note that we are not just talking about the children we come into contact with but also their families, and members of the early years staff team. The early years environment needs to be a welcoming and supportive place for all, and that includes the adults who are there as well as the children. In our book *Gender Diversity and Inclusion in Early Years Education* (Tayler and Price 2016) Kath Tayler and I discuss this at length and this support of staff should also be considered when thinking about the Equality Act, as it is a legal duty of employers as well as good practice.

CASE STUDY 7.2:
SOCIAL SITUATIONS

A group of early years staff are out at a restaurant for an evening social meal at the end of term. They are discussing some children who attend the nursery and one room leader remarks on a little boy who especially likes to dress in the sparkly sari in the dressing-up box. She is his key worker and you overhear her commenting, 'I know that his father isn't happy with it and I don't blame him. It's odds on that he's going to grow up that way, you know.' Some of the other members of the group look uncomfortable and one of them looks pointedly at you, waiting to see your reaction.

What can you do?

You could choose to confront the member of staff at that point and ask them, 'What do you mean by that? He might grow up to be gay? What would be wrong with that?' There are a range of outcomes here. The staff member could say that they didn't mean anything and that this is out of work time anyway and they can say what they think. They could be defensive and say that you misheard them. They could even apologise and say that it was the wine talking. The point is that you would not be prepared for this encounter and to tackle this in such an exposed forum with the rest of the staff looking on might not be the best way to deal with the incident. Equally the rest of the team need to know that you will talk about this in the future and that they can be reassured that their feeling that the staff member should not be talking in this way was correct.

REFLECTION
One way of dealing with this is to say lightly. 'Oh, that's a topic for another day's discussion,' to ensure that everyone is aware that you have heard

the comment and mean to challenge it at some point. Another suggestion would be to ignore the issue when it happens, but in both cases you would need to make some time at work to talk to the staff member privately and challenge them about the conversation. A starting point could be about confidentiality and discussing children and their families in such an open way in public. This could be followed up by a chat with the father concerned so that he could air his worries and think about what he is actually worried about. Finally, it may be appropriate to arrange the next staff meeting to include some in-house training on attitudes towards LGBT issues using the Stonewall (2016) pack (http://www.stonewall.org.uk/sites/default/files/getting_started_toolkit_-_primary.pdf) or ideas from this book. Again, this would give the rest of the staff team the message that such comments need discussion. They might have been made in social time but they reveal attitudes that could impact on the nursery (Tayler and Price 2016, p.5).

Conclusion

I hope that this chapter has given you an insight on how to support the children, parents and carers and staff members who identify as trans or LGB, or who are exploring their gender identity in your setting.

The first most important point to take away from this discussion is that you need to think about these issues and debate as a staff team how you would provide support. As a setting it is best to be prepared for circumstances and to be in the position of being ready, willing and able to give support when it is needed. This is more useful than being reactive – waiting for a situation to reveal itself and then wondering what you are going to do.

The second important point is to remember that you are putting into place the underpinning values and role models for the adult that the child will become. Your actions today will be their memories of tomorrow and you want those memories to be positive ones!

This chapter is just the start of the ongoing discussions and debates that should be happening in your staff team. Remember that it is OK to disagree with someone and to have conflict. Better that than artificial harmony where staff members are operating with a variety of different ideals and values and not providing a cohesive and united programme of support and practice. Through open discussion and the resolution of conflict you will be able to provide a safe and supportive space where children will see adults role-model how to have harmony and disagreement but still work as a cohesive team.

Chapter 8

CONCLUSION

I want to end this book by reflecting on how I began it. I asked the question, why should there be a book on gender diversity and sexuality in the early years and why is this practice important?

Case Study 8.1, which answers this question, is from a recent training that I did.

CASE STUDY 8.1: GROWING UP

This is a very interesting activity to do with a staff team as it raises intersecting and reflective discussion.

As a warm-up exercise I asked the students (17 early years workers only including one man), when they were little what did they want to be when they grew up? It was a mixed student group in terms of age, ranging from their early twenties to their fifties.

The answers started to come: teacher, hairdresser, nurse, cleaner, and netball player – we had one scientist, and the sole man in the group wanted to be a train driver. After the session, while packing up, a student mused, 'Isn't it funny how all of us women chose these types of professions?' and it made me think that the age difference hadn't made any difference – that 99 per cent of the women there, as young children, had aimed to take on a stereotypically female role when they grew up.

REFLECTION

As a young woman at school in the 1960s my career options seemed limited to secretary, shop girl, possibly teacher, nurse and definitely mother. I felt sad that this seemed to be continuing to the present day. It was ironic that on the same day we carried out this exercise thousands and thousands of women worldwide were taking to the streets to march in protest at Donald Trump's inauguration in the USA as he had publicly made statements on many occasions that showed the low esteem he had of women and their place in society.

It didn't escape my notice as well that the one man in the group had wanted to be a train driver – again, a stereotypical male role – and in fact had ended up caring for under-fives in a preschool.

It sounds hackneyed to say 'Children are our future' and yet I do hope that there comes a time very soon where young children will be able to have future dreams that break out of the roles that society seems to have prepared for them.

No one wants children and young people who are exploring their identity and sexuality to be bullied. In order to be bullied there have to be bullies and we want to make sure that all children are supported so that they don't bully other children and young people. This kind of practice is crucial for all children. I can't emphasise enough that practitioners and settings shouldn't wait until issues manifest themselves in the setting. It is so important that settings are aware and introduce discussion and the kind of best practice that I suggest so that they can support all children and families.

Final thoughts

As a summary, the most important principles to put into practice after reading this book are:

- Audit your setting – in terms of resources, environment and attitude.
- Be a role model.
- Think about your children and families – are you reflecting them back at them?
- Invest in the future – in working with children of this young age we are setting the blueprint for their future. If they do question their gender and/or sexuality when they are older then they will remember your setting as a safe space where they could explore themselves and their relation to society. If they are exploring it while they are with you then they will experience love and support from the people around them.

And that's really the best that we can give.

Chapter 9

RESOURCES

In this shorter chapter I will present some resources that might be useful in the early years setting. The other chapters of this book also mention resources that could be useful within some of the activities so this chapter needs to be read in conjunction with them.

Of course, resources are only as good as the people who use them, so a word of warning before spending valuable funds on something as expensive as a Persona Doll, for example. I would always advise borrowing an expensive item initially in order to make sure that the staff team are knowledgeable and capable of making the most from it.

I also think that the setting's most valuable resource is its staff team. Staff training should always be the priority when allocating funds. This is because resources can always be borrowed, or acquired for free in some cases. Resources could also be shared with another local setting.

In fact, sharing resources is a good idea with training as well. It is hard for one practitioner to be released to go to a training event and then be expected to return and cascade that training to the rest of the team. They might not present a whole picture, or might be unsure about the material or lack confidence to take the role of trainer, and that's fine – we can't all be good at everything! The answer could be for a few settings to band together and pay for a trainer to come and deliver group training. I would always recommend Stonewall for anything to do with LGBT issues. Their website (www.stonewall.org.uk) includes teaching materials for primary age children and this could be adapted for use in the early years.

Forest schools

Forest schools are very popular at the moment. They are natural environments where children can play and engage with natural elements. The philosophy behind them is very much based on that of Rudolph Steiner, whose ideas underpin the Steiner schools that are running across the world, including the UK.

In Steiner nurseries careful consideration is also given to the impact of everything in the setting's environment on all the senses of a young child. There are no 'hard' corners, no strong colours, and all the furniture and toys are made of natural materials, as is some of the equipment, like beeswax crayons and sheep's fleece. This extends to the outside area where children are encouraged to engage with the natural world in all of its richness and challenges. The natural rhythms of the year are welcomed and celebrated.

I discussed with students whether they thought that forest schools were more inclusive and less binary focused than other settings in terms of gender. Their feelings were that they are really good examples of children operating with equal confidence regardless of gender because the natural elements/resources that they are engaging with are not gender specific.

However, I would also add the caveat that this would very much depend on the attitude of the practitioners. If they expect the girls to be the gatherers and the boys to be the hunters in the activities that they do then although the resources themselves wouldn't be gender specific, the way that they are approached would be. If the girls were not encouraged to get as dirty as the boys then that would be a problem.

Linking to the point above regarding what we expect to see children doing with resources, Jacky Kilvington and Ali Wood (2016) discuss whether as adults we might have biases towards children's play. Do we as practitioners have pre-existing ideas about gender and so screen out the play that doesn't fit with our expectations and strain to see the gendered play that we want to see? I think that this viewpoint is interesting when applied to toys and books. Do settings buy resources that they think that children like and will use in a certain way – this 'way' being defined by our gender expectations?

Books

I would always recommend the booksellers Letterbox Library (www.letterboxlibrary.com) as they celebrate diversity, and all of their books have been scrutinised (I'm a reviewer for them) to ensure that they deliver positive messages to children. There are also many book lists online if a setting is searching for some good books. I also include here a list of books that people have found useful: books that children might use and books that practitioners could find valuable as a general resource.

Books for children

10,000 Dresses by Marcus Ewert (illustrated by Rex Ray)

Are You a Boy or Are You a Girl? by Sarah Savage and Fox Fisher

Be Who You Are by Jennifer Carr

George by Alex Gino

I Am Jazz by Jessica Herthel

Jacob's New Dress by Ian Hoffman (illustrated by Chris Case)

My Princess Boy by Cheryl Kilodavis and Suzanne DeSimone

Who Are You? The Kid's Guide to Gender Identity by Brook Pessin-Whedbee

Books for practitioners/parents

Can I tell you about Gender Diversity? A Guide for Friends, Family and Professionals by C.J. Atkinson

Gender Born, Gender Made: Raising Healthy Gender-Nonconforming Children by Diane Ehrensaft and Tess Ayers

The Gender Creative Child by Diane Ehrensaft

Raising My Rainbow: Adventures in Raising a Fabulous, Gender Creative Son by Lori Duron

Transgender Child: A Handbook for Families and Professionals by Stephanie Brill and Rachel Pepper

Conclusion

Ultimately the staff team are the most important resource that a setting has and any money available for gender and sexuality issues should be invested in their training and understanding as a priority. However, children do need resources and practitioners can also find them useful as a starting point or inspiration for activities and also to provide underpinning background information.

I suggest that these are borrowed whenever possible so that they can be rotated and changed regularly to keep their freshness and appeal. Books especially are easily borrowed from a library. If a setting does want to buy some then I have made recommendations above. There are also some great books with information for adults and these are listed above in this chapter but also in the reference list at the end of this book.

Before buying books I would always read some reviews in order to get a sense of whether the book would be appropriate for the setting. Once purchased then books need to be valued and used rather than languishing in a cupboard. I recommend that book areas are regularly audited to make sure that the books are in good condition and are suitable. Generally it's better to have fewer good-quality books available for children rather than books that are damaged or too well used and of inferior quality. I would also advise that practitioners always read a book themselves before they read it to children so that they can be prepared for any questions that might arise – this applies to all books supplied for children's use and not just ones on gender diversity and similar topics.

My defining message in this chapter is that children deserve well-trained staff and good quality resources.

REFERENCES

Acas (2015) *Equality and Discrimination: Understand the Basics*. London: Acas. Accessed on 21 April 2017 at www. acas.org.uk/media/pdf/d/8/Equality-and-discrimination-understand-the-basics.pdf

Acas (n.d.) The Equality Act 2010. London: Acas. Accessed on 21 June 2017 at www.acas.org.uk/index. aspx?articleid=3017

Department for Education (2014) *Statutory Framework for the Early Years Foundation Stage*. London: Department for Education. Accessed on 21 June 2017 at www. educationengland.org.uk/documents/pdfs/2014-eyfs-statutory-framework.pdf

Early Education (2012) *Development Matters in the Early Years Foundation Stage (EYFS)*. London: Early Education. Accessed on 21 June 2017 at www.foundationyears.org.uk/files/2012/03/Development-Matters-FINAL-PRINT-AMENDED.pdf

Gill, R. (2006) *Theory and Practice of Leadership*. Abingdon: Sage.

Government Equalities Office (2011) *The Equality Act, Making Equality Real*. Leeds: Government Equalities Office.

Kilvington, J. and Wood, A. (2016) *Gender, Sex and Children's Play*. London: Bloomsbury.

Lyons, K. (2016) 'Childline receives eight calls a day about gender identity issues.' *The Guardian*, 13 December. Accessed on 21 April 2017 at www.theguardian.com/society/2016/dec/13/childline-eight-calls-a-day-gender-identity-issues-children-nspcc-helpline-transgender

NHS Choices (n.d.) Transgender Health. Accessed on 21 June 2017 at www.nhs.uk/Livewell/Transhealth/Pages/Transhealthhome.aspx

Ofsted (2015) *Early Years Inspection Handbook*. Manchester: Ofsted. Accessed on 21 June 2017 at www.gov.uk/government/publications/early-years-inspection-handbook-from-september-2015

Price, D. and Ota, C. (2014) *Leading and Supporting Early Years Teams*. Oxford: Routledge.

Stonewall (2016) *Getting Started: A Toolkit for Preventing and Tackling Homophobic, Biphobic and Transphobic Bullying in Primary Schools*. London: Stonewall.

Strudwick, P. (2014) 'Nearly half of young transgender people have attempted suicide – UK survey.' *The Guardian*, 19 November. Accessed on 21 April 2017 at www.theguardian.com/society/2014/nov/19/young-transgender-suicide-attempts-survey

Tayler, K. and Price, D. (2016) *Gender Diversity and Inclusion in Early Years Education*. Abingdon: Routledge.

INDEX

About the Author

Deborah Price is a senior lecturer at the University of Brighton and an associate lecturer at The Open University. She has worked in early and primary years as a teacher, trainer, inspector and lecturer.